MOVING FORWARD

Leaving My Past Behind Me: A Memoir by Casey Bell

Published by: BookCase Publishing

ISBN-10 0615471927
ISBN-13 9780615471921

Cover Design by Casey Bell

Printed in the United States

Casey Bell
PO Box 5231
Old Bridge, NJ 08857
bookcasepublishing.weebly.com
http://stores.lulu.com/motownbg

CONTENTS

INTRODUCTION

Everyone who knows me can identify me as the color yellow: bright, amusing, sunshiny, happy, wonderful to see, smiley and so much more. I have always been that way it is just natural for me. I think the three words that can describe me the most are quiet, crazy, and funny. It is because of those qualities that I am loved and liked so much. But even in those qualities there are others that I never showed to people because of fear of being hated. I have learned how to hide parts of my life really well. Well enough that even if I told some people what I have done they wouldn't believe it. Due to past events I have been deceived (by Satan and even myself) to begin to take part in a life of lies that has caused me to have low self-esteem, self-hatred, and even suicidal thoughts. I have not only battled seven addictions, but have been in prison and am an "ex-con." With that said I think it is time to get to the beginning of my journey.

THE BEGINNING

The beginning of my story, this story begins at the age of four. I was a boy at age four when I experienced my first sexual experience. I know; that's way too young. I wasn't sure just what to do, but I followed him not knowing it was considered wrong. It was enjoyable and the feelings were all too good. He (let's just call him Dub) was only a year older than me, but my trust in him was the same as a teacher. I trusted in what he was doing. I never thought that he would bring me into an action that is wrong. We got caught a year later and were told that it was wrong and that we should not do such things, but at that moment I already had grown to like it. I felt bad, very guilty because now I knew that what I had liked so much was wrong. It devastated me to know that I couldn't do what I liked to do anymore. However, I quickly learned the best way to do wrong without anyone knowing was to hide it. We continued for years pleasuring each other through sexual contact. It was what I waited for when I saw him. We always made promises that we would stop but we continued. My knowledge was conditioned to know it was wrong, but the knowledge of the pleasure I felt overpowered it. It lasted until I was about eighteen or nineteen years of age. To this day I do not know why it stopped, it just did. We didn't discuss it; it just stopped. But in between the process and even after because of my experience at the age of four I began to unconsciously destroy my life.

DURING THE BEGINNING

The first thing that caused me to destroy my life was when I was about fourteen or fifteen years of age. Actually two separate things happened at two different times in my life. The first thing I remember is seeing pornography for the first time. Dub showed me some pictures he had printed off the internet. They were pictures of naked men posing. It was then that I became fascinated with pornography. The second thing that happened to me was I had officially lost my virginity. It was by accident and I did not realize it until the day I first masturbated. Let me explain. I was about fourteen years and I remember being in bed. I was naked and I was penetrating my penis against my bed. I was pretty much doing what me and Dub did, but because I was alone I used the bed. The feeling was great and at some point (not knowing it would happen) I ejaculated. The feeling was indescribable to me and I wasn't even sure what had happened. I didn't even feel anything exit my penis nor did I see anything. The next day when I awoke I saw the sperm (dried) on my bed, but I had no clue what it was. I simply cleaned it off and never thought about it again (until). I never really knew what masturbation was until Dub told me. Dub told me how to do it. It wasn't until I was alone (without Dub) that I got curious and decided to do it (masturbate). In the end I found out what happens and from the feeling that I received and the "mess" I was able to put two and two together and realize the feeling I felt that night I was on the bed was from masturbation. So it was then that I realized what had happened.

It was also then that I became heavily addicted to pleasuring myself.

ADDICTION NUMBER ONE

The first addiction I ever encountered was an addiction to television. I would watch twelve to twenty hours of television sometimes staying up until five in the morning. I to this day do not know how and why this addiction occurred in my life. But I think it was my escape from being molested. I never had to think about Dub or what we did or how I felt (good and guilty). I would just watch hour upon hour without stopping. I still have not come to a complete conclusion as to why I would watch so much television, but out of all the addictions that I was afflicted with this is the one I conquered the quickest. I simply fasted from it (not watching it for forty days and nights). I did have a relapse, but it wasn't as bad and as of now I watch little to no television. Every day I do not watch television I am shocked that I ever watched that much television and even more shocked that I am able to discipline myself from that addiction. This is one addiction that is 100% conquered.

ADDICTION NUMBER TWO

As crazy as it sounds even though Dub introduced me to porn Dub was not that much into it as I was. In fact it became an addiction for me. I remember being in the car and hearing for the first time a yahoo® commercial. I remember going to the computer and going to yahoo® for the first time and typing in the search bracket "naked men." I went crazy going from website to website looking at these men. I had enjoyed it so much that it became a daily routine. But it didn't end there. I remember in going from website to website stumbling upon a straight sex website and for the first time I saw pictures of heterosexual couples having sex. It was new for me, but I soon became addicted to straight porn. It wasn't just men posing nude, but now straight couples having sex. From there I began to also see threesomes; two women and one man. Usually there was straight and lesbian sex happening in the pictures. From there I stumbled onto female posing websites. At that moment my porn watching was men posing, women posing, straight sex, and threesomes. After seeing the lesbian pictures from the threesomes I got curious and began my first gay search. That was my favorite because it reminded me of what Dub and I would do. In fact at one point I would look at the porn to get new ideas and even new positions for the both of us. Every time we got together I would show him what I learned from the porn. To me it was exciting to do what I had seen from looking at the porn. It seemed like the tables had turned. At the age of four he was teaching me and at the age of fourteen; I was teaching him. Although I was still looking at the previous porn gay porn was my favorite. I even remember looking at porn at school (Middlesex County College) and at the time I did not know the computers were monitored. I got caught and was completely embarrassed. I was out of control. However, it wasn't enough; I had gotten bored with it. I had to keep searching for new porn. From the age of sixteen through about nineteen had discovered a whole variety of porn. I had seen: bestiality, incest, twins, shemales, hermaphrodites, fetishes (feet, bondage, watersports (urination), fisting, role playing, toys), group sex, bisexual, gay, lesbian, straight, black, white, Asian, Hispanic, pregnant women, midgets, foreign, domestic, old, young, and too young. I remember the first time I came to a website and there were naked children. I really got excited then. By then the sex between me and Dub had ended and looking at this porn was a great memory of our past together. It also helped me to stay in denial. As I said before I always felt bad that Dub subjected me to something bad (wrong (sin)). I felt better knowing that what we did together was indeed okay and not in any way bad. So seeing these children with each other and looking like they consented help me to believe that indeed what we (Dub and I) did was okay and is okay. After finding it I became heavily addicted. I began to search and search and search and every time I found more I made sure I did not forget where I found it. I was excited to see this porn everyday. I will admit there was always a side of me that said, "This will not last

forever. I will not continue to look at this porn forever." There were even time

periods where I had stopped looking at it and promised myself I would not look

any more, but the addiction was way to strong and I did not want to give it up. I

had obtained these addictions at an early age and did not want to give up the

pleasure I received. This was just one addiction that kept me stuck in a horrible

state of mind.

ADDICTION NUMBER THREE

It may sound crazy, but the third addiction I had was masturbation. Some people may think there is nothing wrong with self pleasure, but when it controls you then there is something wrong. I did it everyday multiple times a day and when I wasn't doing it I was thinking about doing it. There were even times when I was in school I would go to the bathroom and right there in the stall would go for it. Many times I went into public bathroom stalls (malls, stores, restaurants); it didn't matter just as long no one saw I was okay. I couldn't stop myself. Any time I felt like I needed to do it I would. My favorite thing to do was to masturbate with porn; especially when I upgraded from pictures to video. Watching the videos was so much fun and better than just looking at the pictures. I would watch the videos and imagine myself with someone I was attracted to and enjoy every second of it. Once I was done; every time I was done I would always feel guilty and ashamed of myself. I would always tell myself that I had to stop and take control of myself, but soon memories would fill my head from past pleasures and I would remember how much I enjoyed the feelings and before you know it I was back at that computer searching for more porn. I never liked myself because of it, but I allowed masturbation to control me.

ADDICTION NUMBER FOUR

I believe this was probably the first addiction that I had. When I was a child I was always big and I loved to eat. I basically ate anything and everything and always ate in big proportions. From fifth grade all the way through twelfth grade I was bullied because of my weight. I hated me for being so fat and I would always go on diets that never lasted. I truly believe the reason why I ate so much was because it (food) was my friend when Dub wasn't around. I never felt hungry when I was in pleasure town, but when I was away I ate like crazy. I used food like a pacifier whenever I didn't have Dub's pacifier to pacify me (I hope you know what I mean). I did not realize that at the time. During that time I just did things not realizing I was still a boy in pain from being molested. This to me is still difficult for me to accept. I say that because as I was growing up and learned about molestation, I always identified it as an adult having sex or raping a child. I never saw it as a child molesting another child. But indeed that's what it was. I never at that time realized what I was going through because I was still excited about the pleasure I was receiving. I never thought that emotional pain would be produced neither did I have any knowledge that I would be addicted to any of these things. Either or along with porn, and masturbation, food was another addiction in my life.

CAUGHT RED-HANDED

So at the age of nineteen Dub and I had ended our sexual relationship. I do not know why it ended. We never discussed ending it we just did. Every time we met we had sex at least once. Usually more than once. But one day he came over and nothing happened. And since that day we never had sex again. I was still heavily addicted to porn, food, and because my sex life had ended I was masturbating even more. It was then at the age of twenty that I did something completely stupid, but to make a long story short one day in January in the year of 2003 the police were at the door and I was at the police station arrested for uploading and downloading child porn. At this moment I thought my life was over and I would never be able to do anything ever again. As I was sitting there answering their questions I was hoping it was a nightmare and that I would wake up. The one thing that made me very angry was the fact that the police officers (two of them) openly lied to me. Their exact words were, "If you tell us everything we will let you go (back home) and we will make sure the judge knows you cooperated with us." So my dumb-ass told them everything and from there I wasn't at home I was in jail. I was angry that they lied to me so much that I quickly became a cop hater. I was signing those 1980's hip-hop cop killer songs. But I was angrier with myself for talking to those cops. I soon was in prison and very afraid. I kept to myself and said as less as I could. Soon I was transferred to another part of the prison nd was even more afraid. The one thing I hated the most about prison is how

osy everyone is. Everyone kept asking me what I was in for and I wanted to say

one of your business, but I was too passive for that. People were nice to me, but

oon all that crap I told the police was in the newspaper and the prisoners came to

ny bed and was angry with me. It was at that point I had wished I lied to them

when they asked me my name. I was really afraid I was going to get either beat or

aped, but thank God for His protection. After being bullied (verbally) by

ypocrites (wrong is wrong, never think your wrong is less than someone else's. If

ou are in jail and know you are guilty you have no right condemning anyone else)

I kept to myself and decided not to eat. I went on a fast (it was supposed to help

me change, but it didn't). I began that day in prison a "forty days forty nights"

fast and it was soon that I was bailed out and I was too happy.

COMING HOME

After being bailed out I was happy to be out of prison, but too ashamed to see anyone. I did not want anyone to see me and really I just wanted to die. When I went back to church they welcomed me with warm arms. I hated it though. Knowing they knew what I did. I was hiding it all that time and now it was all out in the open. Not all, but many of my family members knew what happened and even they still loved me. It was nice to know that I was loved, but I still hated what I had done and I hated that they knew. From being in prison I had missed the first week of school (college). I returned for my second semester at Kean University petrified. Thankfully the newspaper article was in a different county than Kean, but I still wasn't sure who knew about me. So I hated (and even to this day) to say my name afraid they were (will) notice it from the newspaper article. I spent basically the rest of my Kean years in fear, but to my knowledge no one knew or at least they just did not bring it up. Actually I believe at least three people (students I knew from high school) knew, but never mentioned it. I had a great time at Kean, a wonderful time, really, but things only got worse (the addictions).

COURT ORDER

While I was in the process of being convicted (I plead guilty) I was ordered by the court to have counseling. I spent a little over a year and $150 a session with a psychiatrist. I hated every session because they weren't working. Mostly my fault, but he would basically ask the same questions each time; and because I still wasn't ready to give up the addictions. I was still looking at porn, masturbating, and well I will get to the eating later. I did not look at child porn, but I continued to look at all the other porn previously mentioned. I did abstain from masturbating for a period of time, but soon caved in and went for it for the first time in a long time. So, I felt pretty bad lying to the doctor because he would ask me if I was abstaining from the porn and masturbation and I would say yes, knowing the answer was no. It was at that point that I wasn't so upset at the police anymore because I had just realized those lies they told me was just what I reaped (from me lying to my mother about porn). My mother asked me many times if I was looking at porn on the computer (prior to being arrested) and I always denied it. So it is really true; what goes around comes around. And it came around hard. So any way I never thought that I would ever have to get help from a shrink, but there I was on the couch talking about my life and fears to a man I really did not trust; and I did not care to be there and I just wanted my life to end.

ADDICTION NUMBER FIVE

During my second semester at Kean I was still on my fast. I had noticeably (to everyone but me) lost a lot of weight. I really wasn't noticing the weight I was losing I was just fasting, hoping to get rid of those addictions. I know the only reason why I did not lose the addictions along with the weight was because I wasn't praying as much and I just had this grip on my past. I just could not let go of what Dub and I did and I could not let go of the feelings I felt with him. So anyway, as I finished the fast addiction number four began. Once I began to eat again many, many, many people who saw my weight change began to commit and I begin to slowly, surely notice my weight change. Although my body wasn't perfect it was better than it was prior to the fast. But it was because my body wasn't perfect that I began addiction number four. I began to think "if I lost weight from not eating I can lose the rest the same way." So it was than that I began to fast some more. By then it was getting easier not to eat and pas it off as fasting. People than began to get a little concerned, but I always told them don't worry I am okay. My fasting sessions turned into anorexia. I would stop eating for long periods of time an only eat when I was with people so they would not think I was anorexic. And because of fear of being found out addiction number six was created.

ADDICTION NUMBER SIX

As I was in Kean I took a playwriting course in the English department. My final project was a play about a boy who had bulimia. Because I did not have much knowledge of it I went online and did some research. I thought the only action of bulimia was vomiting, but I soon found out that some use laxatives soon after eating to keep from gaining the weight. That idea was great to me because I never liked vomiting. So about four months later I brought my first bottle of laxatives and every time I ate I used a laxative. It was a heavy addiction because I did it every day after every meal sometimes even when I was "fasting" I would use laxatives. I then even began to buy laxative teas and fiber pills and was doing everything I could think of to get rid of everything I ate that day. I never thought that I would be bulimic or even anorexic. And to make things worst addiction number three returned. Any time I got really hungry I would scarf down big amounts of food, but I would put my mind at ease knowing that I had laxatives. I was completely messed up. I would shuffle from over-eating to bulimia to anorexia time and time again and I hated it. I hated that I had no self-discipline and very low self-esteem. I battled these three food addictions every day.

THE JUDGE'S FINAL SAY

After the whole ordeal of being arrested; in August 2003 the judge ordered me to three years probation. The probation consisted of continuing to see the doctor and abstaining from porn. He did this because I was in school and because I was doing well he decided to not put me in prison. However, being that this was August I was put into prison up until school started which ended up being ten days (not bad at all considering). I thank God for that because I truly believe it was him who kept me from serving three years in prison. Then again having this record on my name I really didn't think it made a difference. Having this record on my name caused me to hate everything about me and everything I had done up until then. My life was full of regret and I was wishing every day and every night to redo at least the last three years. I just wanted to change some things in my life, but I knew I couldn't. I hated me because I had caused a huge problem in my life. Job struggles.

JOB STRUGGLES

graduated Kean in 2005 with all addictions attached to me. I was still searching or porn I was still masturbating and I was still battling between the three food ddictions. I had left college and I struggled to hold down a job. I hated myself ecause every job application I filled out I had to put that I was an ex-con. To this day I haven't been able to get a sustainable job and I hated myself because of it. veryone sees a person like me as disgusting, perverted and untrustworthy, but no ne ever tries to understand why one would even enjoy child porn. No one ever hinks that maybe this person is damaged and rejecting him/her is not they way to ix him/her. But I am over people judging me. I cannot change the past so there vill be forever someone hating me for what I have done. After college I got a job t McDonald's and a live theatre (still employed part-time), but I was never able o get "the job." My dream job is to work in the entertainment business, but have vet to step in. The topic of this chapter has led me (many times) to thinking it night be better if I was "not to be." It just made sense at the time. I hated me, veryhing I had done (child porn, arrested, etc.), and of course the addictions. To this day I always hated people asking me what I did (for a living). I never liked my answers; I enjoyed my jobs, but they were not what I wanted. I hated my job struggles and was the top reason why I was ready to leave this earth.

ADDICTION NUMBER SEVEN

As if I needed anymore I invited another addiction into my life. Well, not so much another addiction, I resurrected one. As said before by the age of nineteen I was not having sex anymore. Although I dreamed of it with other people I was attracted to it never actually happened. I believe it was around 2007 that I was on craigslist® looking for a job (never found one yet) and I saw personals. I curiously looked at them and saw an opportunity. Although afraid I went ahead and contacted my first sex partner (other than Dub). We emailed each other and than made a date. It was a Wednesday. I drove to his place and he invited me in. I will admit it was good. It brought back great pleasurable memories from when I was just a little boy. I missed the one on one contact and meeting with this guy (Man #1) was great. Man #2 had a girlfriend and children. The pictures were in his room. I did not know that at the time we chose to meet, but I was there so we went for it. He had asked me to come back before his girlfriend came home, but I did not. Man #3 was a construction worker. We had sex in the house that he was working on. Man #4 was about sixty years of age. I met up with after work. Although he was up in age he was fun. Man #5 was divorced and his son was in school when we met. I think we were supposed to meet again, but we never did. I met up with Man #6, but nothing happened. He wanted to meet first so we met at a food court and talked. He never contacted me after so we never had the chance to have sex. Man #7 I met at an adult bookstore. The bookstore had video booths. It is very normal there to invite a man (men) in and to sexual pleasure each other. It's against the bookstores rules, but people do it anyway. We (Man #7) met up twice and was supposed to meet up a third time, but it didn't happen. Man #8 was 40ish and hairy. The time with him lasted the longest compared to the other men. It had to be about an hour before we finished. Man #9 was Hispanic and barely spoke English. I met him at his house and he pleasured me the whole time. I remember sitting in the dark with the television on; every now and then I would glance at the television. After man number nine it was getting more difficult to book dates so I began to frequent adult bookstores booths and solicited the men (strangers) that were there. I had to come in contact with a total of at least six to seven men while I went. I didn't really care that I had gave myself away to so many men. I was just trying to fulfill (feed) the addiction. I couldn't stop remembering the pleasure Dub gave me and when we stopped I had to get it from some where else. I hated me for what I was doing, but I could not resist the pleasure.

WHAT'S THAT?

I don't know if they were just warning signs from God or what they were, but slowly, but surely I begin to see and feel signs that I might have an (or many) STD(s). I went to the clinic and I was afraid, nervous, and even anxious. They were about six to seven other people there. The clinic was playing a Halle Berry movie. I remember watching it I was waiting to be tested. I felt so irresponsible, guilty, foolish, and stupid for getting to the point where I had to go to the clinic. I hated the fact that I had to answer questions about my sex life because I was ashamed of it (sex life). I never wanted to be identified as gay so telling the nurses that I only had sex with men and what I did was very embarrassing and shameful for me. After being tested for STDs I then went into another room to be tested for HIV/AIDS. There was only one person in there. I went in and the guy asked me more of the same questions and I hated to answer them. In the end I was negative and I was very elated. I then decided to abstain from porn, masturbation, and sex.

HOW LONG WAS THAT?

I cannot tell you how long the abstinent period was, but I can tell you it did not last. I soon began searching for porn again and even though I was not masturbating I soon began to do that once again. Later I began to frequent the adult bookstores once again. I hated me every time, but I couldn't help myself. I began "fasting" again as well. And it was about maybe two to three years of being free from bulimia, but I soon brought another bottle of laxatives. I couldn't understand why these addictions had me bound so well. Nothing I did helped me break free. I know it was because in my mind I did not want to give them up. I had these addictions two of them as early as the age of four. The pleasure I felt always reminded me to keep looking for sex and porn, and the guilt wasn't strong enough to stop me. Every day was a battle. Some days I went without them and some days were filled with them. Some days I continued to evaluate whether or not I was worth living. I hated me, my life, and everything I was doing. But no matter how much self-hatred I inflicted I still continued with the pain of these addictions. "Why can't you stop," is what I would always ask myself and never could find an answer. The one thing that really made me hate myself was that I went five years without looking at child porn and yet I still allowed that addiction to make me look once again. Every moment I looked fear filled my bones. I was afraid I was going to get caught a second time. But even the thought of being arrested did not stop me. I hated myself even the more because again I was hiding

and being one person inside and another outside. I was Dr. Jekyll and Mr. Hyde

for real. And all I ever wanted was to go back to the age four to redo my life.

Because then maybe it wouldn't be filled with these addictions.

MY LAST MAN

My last sexual encounter was with a man I met from craigslist®. After I posted an

d he contacted me and we soon met. I came to his house and for the first time in

 while I had another sexual encounter. I enjoyed it, but I hated it. Let me

eword that; my flesh enjoyed it, but my spirit hated it. We met a total of three

imes (the most I ever met up with the same man) and each time it got better.

Pleasure is a difficult thing because it feels right, but sometimes is wrong. That's

what kept me confused my whole addicted life. I knew every addiction was wrong,

but the pleasure or the good outcome is what kept me feeding them. I think the

best thing about having sex with this man was that fact that he was completely

discrete. Most gay men or men who identify themselves as a gay man do not like it

when men are discrete about sex. They think all men who have sex with men

should be out of the closet. But I never considered myself as gay only molested. I

never wanted love, marriage, rights; I just wanted to feel good. I wanted the

pleasure Dub introduced to me when I was four to last forever. I did not want it to

end. I did not want a long term relationship or anything of the sorts. I just

wanted the pleasure to be everlasting. So being with him was great because I

could be pleasured and be discrete with him. But at the same time I knew at some

point it would have to end. And I knew as soon as it ended with him he would

have to be the last.

NOT TO BE

After scanning my life and seeing how much of a hell it was I began to question it. I realized that I could not get a decent job because of my prison record. Every audition I went to I was rejected. Every business venture I created staggered and made no profits. Everything I tried to do seemed to fail (accept the addictions). I just could not see any reason to keep living. I really got to the point where I told God I think it is time for me to come home (Heaven). I was afraid though because I thought to myself there is a chance I might not make it to Heaven. And I do not like too much heat so it took me a long time to actually come to the conclusion of suicide. But on one day I decided that with everything in my life going sour, bitter, cold, bad, everything but good, it was time to leave. So, as I began to ponder how I was going to end my life I asked God if he could give me just one reason to stay on Earth, I would stay, but if He couldn't that I was ready to go home. He then said, "If you kill yourself it is going to be pretty difficult for your siblings to tell your nephews and nieces why they can never see their Uncle Casey again. I then stopped in my tracks and began to sob. I was so selfish that I completely forgot about my nephews and nieces. I thought about everyone else and thought that they didn't need me, but I didn't even think of them. I was angry, depressed, and ashamed of thinking of suicide all at the same time. I was a wreck that day. I soon picked up the pieces and moved on. I was still upset because I knew I did not conqueror the addictions as of yet. I asked God why I am

still feeling this way. God had answered me by telling me about the boy in a man.

BOY IN A MAN

Although I had grown each year physically it was around 2010 that I realized I was still a four year old boy. The day I was molested was the day I died and never grew a day older. I did not know that during my journey. I did not realize my whole life of addictions was produced through me being molested. I did not have the knowledge in knowing if I would have just confessed and repented and dealt with my past I would have been a better person. Live a better life. It was this revelation that had me crying many days simply because I could not stop from being killed. I never had the chance to tell that four year old do not agree to being molested. There were days that I wished that me as an adult could have told me as a boy what not to do. I always get angry with everyone talking about safe sex and "wrap it up" and all that crap. I get angry when people do not emphasize abstinence and celibacy. I get angry when people talk about their first time and giving it up because I never had the chance to give it. Mine was taken. Even though I was having sex I would always tell people to abstain because I wanted them to get the chance to freely by their own choice give their virginity. I never wanted people regretting their choices like I did. I really wish more organizations were more vocal about abstinence and being a proud virgin rather than safe sex. I only wish I had the choice to be a virgin today. I would love to, but I cannot. In this time is when I began to realize that I had to forgive that four year old. I had to realize it wasn't his fault that he didn't say no. I had to deal with him in order to resurrect him and grow him into a man. It was not easy because I had to finally step out of denial mode and confess to myself that the sex I had and was having although felt glorious was indeed wrong. I had to confess to myself that feeding myself food, porn, and laxatives could never heal me from the pain of the dead four year old boy. I had to stop lying to myself that it was okay to look at child porn. I had to stop allowing the porn to be my reason for continuing to be molested. I had actually realized that every time I had sex that it wasn't me, but that four year old boy that never got healed. It may sound crazy but sometimes the truth sounds worse than a lie. But I knew the lies that I was feeding me was only going to put me back into deeper trouble. I had realized it was either deal with the truth and live or continue living with the lies and die. Today I have conquered the food addictions, but I am still in battle with LUST (porn, masturbation, and sex). Everyday I have to continue to deal with the four year old boy who never got the chance to live. I have to remember that he is not the age he should be yet and it is my duty to get him there.

IT'S NOT OVER YET

Although this is the end of the book my journey is not over yet. I just had to get this load off of my back. Hiding can be exhausting at times and I knew the only way I could expose my past successfully without lying was to put it on paper. I know I will be judged, but I have finally come beyond fearing what people may or may not think of me. Thanks to a friend's quote I have finally figured out, "What people think of me is none of my business." So I write this memoir not only for me, but for you. For if we indeed do not have the right to cast stones I am sure there are some things you may be hiding too. And maybe, just maybe this will encourage you to come out of hiding and tell it all. I think it is the time that we make every season a season for confession. Not in a booth, but in the open like the bible says. And as we remember that no one is perfect (even ourselves) that we not judge one another for our past mistakes. And even come to the conclusion that we need not measure our mistakes; because your mistakes are not less or more than mine and vice versa. We as a human race should be the ones to help each other conqueror the addictions instead of judge each other because of the addictions. In conclusion, my story is just one of many and I know I am not the only one who has a four year old boy (5, 6, 7, 8, 9, boy/girl) stuck inside of him/her. Let us all grow him/her up. Deal with the broken child within. Grace and peace be unto you.

CPSIA information can be obtained
at www.ICGtesting.com
Printed in the USA
LVHW101300150623
749880LV00004B/67